A Mother of Sons

poems of love, wisdom & dreams

Jayne Jaudon Ferrer

LOYOLAPRESS.

CHICAGO

LOYOLAPRESS.

3441 N. ASHLAND AVENUE
CHICAGO, ILLINOIS 60657
(800) 621-1008
WWW.LOYOLABOOKS.ORG

A previous edition of this book was published by
Pocket Books in 1996.

Cover illustration: Clifford Alejandro
Cover and interior design by Megan Duffy Rostan

Library of Congress Cataloging-in-Publication Data

Ferrer, Jayne Jaudon.
  A mother of sons : poems of love, wisdom, & dreams / Jayne Jaudon
Ferrer.
     p. cm.
  ISBN 0-8294-1770-2
  1. Mothers and sons—Poetry. 2. Motherhood—Poetry.
3. Boys—Poetry. 4. Men—Poetry. I. Title.
  PS3556.E72578M68 2004
  811'.54—dc22

                                          2003014830

Printed in the United States
03 04 05 06 07 M-V 10 9 8 7 6 5 4 3 2 1

For James, who reminds me to
appreciate every day,
and for Jaron, who makes me laugh.

Contents

Acknowledgments

When is a collection of poetry like a box of laundry detergent? When it's "New and Improved!" If you liked the first edition of this book, you're gonna love this one. I've polished and tweaked, found a better word here, a stronger image there, and I've added a few new tales that I've lived to tell. (When you're a mother of sons, that's no small feat.) Illustrated in a distinctive new style and available where it hasn't been before, this edition promises to bring untold levels of sympathy and understanding from the world to those of us raising boys.

I'm grateful to my sister, Vera Stanfield, for her unfailing encouragement and support; she is everything a big sister should be—except close by. I appreciate my friends Kelly Arledge, Laura Gould, Catherine Ritch Guess, Amy Nottingham, Joan Schauder, and Carlynne Smith, who know firsthand the rigors and rewards of life in a household of males. I appreciate my husband's faith and flexibility. And I really, *really* appreciate my sons' tolerance of my need to turn life (theirs, in particular) into a poetic experience. My thanks, also, to Deb DiSandro and Marianne Gingher for their kind evaluation and enthusiasm.

The loyalty of my readers and your affection for this book have amazed me. I'm so pleased that my words manage to capture what you feel. I know every time I go back and reread one of these poems, it's like getting to relive that moment all over again—not always easy to do, especially as our little boys grow into men—but always a sweet, sweet experience. (Well, not always. I frankly would like to immediately eliminate from my memory bank *all* moments upon which "Student Driver" was based.)

Thank you for reading, for writing, for remembering; may your life overflow with the blissful bedlam that only boys can bring!

J.J.F.

Exuberant Sons

"Mom, I love you sixty-seven fifty. Is that a lot?"

—Jaron, age four

Rudiments of Life

If I could give you a list of ways
to make your life more pleasant,
I would say
eat mangoes,
stand tall,
pick apples,
read books,
buy flowers,
smell stew,
give presents,
get hugs,
bake cookies,
write letters,
pet puppies,
climb mountains,

wear sweaters,
hear music,
make friends,
use chopsticks,
go skiing,
hold babies,
fly kites,
watch clouds,
sing passionately,
breathe deeply,
attend church,
eschew politics,
acquire patience,
ignore idiots,
pray daily,

cry unashamedly,
smile freely,
laugh lustily,
be truthful,
share knowledge,
ask questions,
take naps,
plan picnics,
kiss gently,
say thank you,
save keepsakes,
celebrate often,
love lots.

The Boys Club

We know who we are.
Ours is like one of those
ancient, fraternal orders
whose identifying rituals include
elaborate hand signals and
mysterious primal grunts.
In public,
the cue is often a series
of short, repetitive barks:
"Sit *down!*"
"Give me that!"
"Come *here!*"
"NOW!"
People who aren't in the club
look disdainful, annoyed,
disgusted, or smug.

But fellow members grin—
slowly at first, as they
identify and empathize—
then broadly, as they
catch your eye and
nod slightly to acknowledge
well-known phrases and
familiar responses.
"Boys are somethin', aren't they?"

Attack of the Diapered Viking

I hear it once again.
The staccato breaths,
impatient panting,
and pawing palms.
Then finally comes
the valiant growl
of conquest—
"Aiiiiiiiiiihhh!"—
and I watch,
bemused,
as once again you plunge forth
in unflinching pursuit
of the notorious lamp cord.

Fair skin, fiery curls, and
full diaper firmly in place,
you look like Erik the Red
come to vanquish a port.
Is this the spirit
with which you'll go forth
to conquer the world?
If it is, dear boy,
the battle's already fought;
the victory, yours!

Midnight Rendezvous

It is with something less than
maternal goodwill that I crawl,
asleep and annoyed,
from my coveted bed
to silence your angry screams
violating the night.
We rock in the chair
that has been ours since
the very beginning,
ensconced in
Great-Grandmother's afghan and
the VCR's ghostly green light.
Mute now, but for
periodic, pitiful whimpers,
you cling to me like some
abandoned creature reclaimed.

Clinging back,
I am EveryMother,
an all-knowing, all-bestowing,
all-loving, all-forgiving
paragon of matriarchal perfection.
Feeling your sweet, soundless breaths
tease the tangles of hair
on the back of my neck,
my last trace of irritation
over interrupted sleep
dissipates in a hug, a kiss,
and a smile.
You will never remember
these midnight moments together;
I will never forget.

Mother Lode

Like porpoises frolicking
on a perfect, sun-streaked day or
fat puppies practicing fun, but
unfamiliar, roles,
we squeal and growl and
clutch and collide in time
to no one's rhythm but our own.
Shrieking, you fall on my face,
openmouthed,
with ardor and wet kisses
no college boy could ever hope
to top.
Smiling,
I seize five of those twenty
tiny, tireless tips/toes,

the ones that never seem
to still themselves for an instant,
then consume them,
piece by piece,
in savoring chomps.
How marvelous to explore
the wonder of each other,
unencumbered
by consequence or clocks!
We are two
in a private universe of discovery,
each new find a fuse
for tomorrow's adventures.

Word Pictures

Denim and boots,
white Sunday suits,
kisses and giggles,
wet beds and wiggles.
Monsters and fables,
climbing on tables,
baseballs and bats,
pulled tails of cats.
Crayons and mud,
bruises and blood,
guns, forts, and sticks,
"Voila!" magic tricks.

Video games,
hot cars and airplanes,
back talk and bragging,
car keys and nagging.
Acne and hair creams,
night jobs and daydreams,
tuition and classes,
mascaraed lashes.
Resumes, rings;
he's spreading his wings.
My little boy's gone;
how time marches on!

I Am a Mother of Sons

I am a mother of sons—
robust boys with curly hair
and sunburst smiles
and a penchant for ice cream
and frogs.

I am a mother of sons—
pale boys with velvet eyes
and contemplative souls
and not enough time
to do nothing.

I am a mother of sons—
dark boys with gentle hearts
and troubled minds
and spirits that sprint back
inexplicably.

I am a mother of sons—
frail babes with frantic cries
and feeble grips
who dare not imagine
tomorrow.

I am a mother of sons—
proud boys with shoulders squared
who, nobly, stood for
democracy's sake,
fell heroes on foreign soil.

I am a mother of sons—
humble men whose blood
purged the souls of all sons,
whose love will engulf us
forever.

Eager Sons

Boys are much better than girls, 'cause they can fight, and be ninjas, and dance cool, and burp.

—James, age five

The Best Intentions

I don't believe in
treating all children alike.
So I bought
one dinosaur place mat,
one alphabet place mat,
and one with a map of the world.

I've decided
children shouldn't have place mats.
And, if they do,
they should all be
plain white.

Welcome to My World

There is no pink in my house—
just a rough-ridged rainbow of
red, yellow, and blue Legos
(and guns—not real ones, not even toy ones,
just imaginary ones that began life
as azalea twigs and shoe horns)
that encrust my carpet
and spread like
alley cat kudzu.
Battle cries.
War whoops.
Raucous laughter.
Loud burps.

Silence, if it comes,
sits only long enough for mealtime grace.
Even then, testosterone rears its rowdy head:
Me do it!
No, *me!!*
No, me!!!
Thanks get returned in triplicate
at eighty decibels and ninety miles an hour,
as each one tries to make sure
his words
get to God
first.

Perspective

My heart breaks when I hear the words:
"Mommy, am I bad?"
O, vile tongue!
You who have mocked this child
with your sarcasm,
screamed at his pint-sized destruction,
threatened his very existence.
O, hateful hand!
You who have shaken in anger
that head of bright curls,
slapped outstretched arms
that refused to withdraw,
pointed the way to exile
down the hall.
O wounded heart!
This, my challenge child,
the one who
daily

takes me to the edge of tolerance
then yanks me back into
a canyon of love,
who engineers feats of abject desecration
beyond my wildest conjuring,
while oozing preciousness and
precociousness and
plain old irresistible
spunkiness
from every sweet, sweaty,
little boy pore.
No, my darling,
you are not bad!
You are overwhelmingly
wonderful.

A Day in the Life

Mom, he hit me!
He pushed me!
I had that ball first!
That airplane is mine!
Mom, make him stop!
I'm telling!
He won't share!
It's my turn!
Mom, he's not being fair!
I don't have to!
He's messing everything up!
You're gonna be in trouble!
Mom, come *here!*
I'm not playing with you anymore!
I mean it!
You're stupid!
Mom, he said a bad word!
Did not!
Did, too!
You jerk-head!

Mom, I'm bored!
This is no fun!
Can we come out of time-out now?
We'll play outside!
We promise!
Thanks, Mom!

Mom, he hit me!
He pushed me!
I had that toy first!
That stick is mine!
Mom, make him stop!
I'm telling!
You jerk-head!

Cowboy Cookies

It was on the way to Grandma's,
I think.
Entrepreneurial embers flaming,
desperate for something to do
besides counting birds or
listening to (heaven forbid!) Barney again,
you actually worked together
peacefully—
even pleasantly!—
and "Cowboy Cookies" were born.
Casing the billboards on I-75,
you concede competition is tough.
But what kid could resist,

you reasoned,
cowboys and horses and hats
served up in three favorite flavors?
By the time we got there,
you'd gone from cookies
to complete cuisine:
"Pow Wow Pancakes," "Hiawatha Hot Dogs,"
"Cone Rangers," and "Silver Sundaes."
You guys still laugh and recall that trip
once in a while;
the memory is still
delicious
after all these years.

About Sundays

(or Why the Future of Formal Religious Services
Is in Peril for Families of Small Children)

The good ones
are when nobody spills grape jelly
on the front of a clean shirt Mom just ironed,
and everybody goes straight to the car
without chasing the dog or
going after a bug or
jumping . . .
"Uh-oh!" . . .
over a puddle,
and somebody doesn't yell, "Oh, no!
I forgot my money for *Jesus!!!*"
at the top of his lungs
right in front of the Esther Class window
just after they've bowed for prayer.

The bad ones
are when somebody thinks the preacher's
rhetorical questions
require earnest, honest,
clearly enunciated answers,
and everybody waves at Dad in the choir loft,
and in sign language
loud enough to reach Borneo,
points out their own exemplary behavior,
and the very rude antics of their siblings,
and nobody has a clue why
Mom feels a headache coming on
every Saturday night.

Lesson Review

Have I taught you the right things,
my darlings?
Between laundry and table-setting,
ironing and pants-hemming,,
manners and morals and
where to pin the corsage,
did I remember to teach about love?
About listening and hearing
and holding and helping
and *always remembering* to put down the toilet seat?

While I ferried you to school and soccer,
band and sleepovers,
birthdays and baseball and church,
did I find time to talk about life?
About philosophy and philanthropy
and ethics and art
and *never* leaving before the credits have run?

There's just so much that matters!
You must know about
politics, heretics,
deferment, fulfillment,
pain, civic duty,
civil rights, inner beauty . . .

Oh, I want to teach you everything, darlings!
But life is so brief; its wonders so vast.
And there's no textbook for
Teaching Life (or How to Turn Boys into Men).
I'll just keep telling you all I can think of;
you just keep asking me
what's on
The Test.

Earnest Sons

Hasn't this been just the bestest day?

—John, age three

Almanac

It is summer.
I know from wild, primal whoops that
echo
in the afternoon stillness.
From firm-fleshed rumps
glistening
like peaches in the breeze
as one, two, *three!* they
bounce
in front yard sprinklers and backyard pools.
I know from sweat-damp foreheads
and blackberry-moist chins,
chubby hands
clenched
around pickle jars blinking
    twi-light
        twi-light
            twi-i-i-light
in the cabernet softness.

It is fall.
I know from dancing eyes and
cinnamon cheeks that
peek
over smiling wisps of cocoa.
From cowboy boots
scuffling
through restless crimson and topaz leaves
like tiny torpedoes
streaking
into a school of skittish guppies.
I know from pumpkins,
their smooth flesh
hacked
and jagged where virgin fingers
sought to create ghouls
from a simple gourd.

It is winter.
I know from giddy whispers
in the halls,
carillon giggles that rival cherished carols
in their sweet, simple melodies of joy.
From fingertips frosted
pink as a newborn kitten's nose,
their woolly red cocoons
flung aside
in pursuit of the perfect snowball.
I know from
footsteps
in the final chill before dawn ascends,
a prelude to softly rooting heads and
feebly flailing limbs in search of
warmth and safe haven
for a few moments more.

It is spring.
I know from
sweaters slung
impatiently
around slim denim hips,
the sole concession made
to still-brisk mornings.
From lace—Queen Anne's—
pieceworked
with just-plucked stems of milkweed and
    black-eyed Susans
presented in a pride-filled fist.
I know from bunnies,
chocolate ones and
plush ones and
terrified ones
clutched in smudged, impetuous arms
I hope will always make room
for me.

Carpe Diem

You, middle child of mine—
whose heart do you have?
(Mine, of course; you stole it
years ago.)
But whose *are* you?
Affectionate, quick-witted,
awash in joie de vivre . . .
you stand, stalwart, with arms open wide,
welcoming each moment of life
like a long-lost friend.
I envy your aplomb—
applaud it!—
and ponder which ancestor's
congenial gene pool deserves credit
for your
indefatigable energy level.

Command Performance

It's when he sings to me
I ache for time to stop.
Just-cut blond bangs
framing a face so pure
it seems straight from heaven.
The notes come softly—
giggle-laced and laden with pride—
as familiar tunes
meander valiantly
through still-awkward syllables.

While the older ones
roll eyes in bored disgust,
I am rapt,
on fire with love,
tears a mere pulse away from my smile as, frenzied,
my heart records every image
from eyelash to hiccup.
I'll want to replay this moment
someday,
after this show has closed
to make way for the next.

Kindred Spirits

You, eldest son,
with the face of your father,
the grin of your granddad,
are mine.

In your eyes,
I see myself—
searching for secrets,
summoning truth,
sizing up acceptance
with a cool gray gaze.

Spirit clones, we—
fueled by images
     and words
     and wonderment
long after others
have bid day adieu.

The world is different
during onyx hours;
silent, serene, uncensored—
the time when our souls speak loudest,
the time when our hearts hear best.

Earth Angel

You, my youngest one—
lover of music,
champion of animals,
jubilant night sprite who never sleeps—
I long to know what lies ahead for you.

Feisty, yet fragile,
intent on achieving, come what may,
you trudge on
long after the rest of us fade or
fall dormant.
That twinkle in your eye,
that twitch in your dashing dimple—
are they part of the magic that makes you
so bold and invincible?

I know!
You are an angel,
bequeathed to earth when heaven's fair host
could no longer entertain
or sustain you.

Swing Time

Here we go, looby-loo,
here we go, looby-lie.
Here I go pushing you
all the way up to the sky!

Watching you swing
is my favorite thing.
Pure joy,
reckless abandon.
Reaching for heaven,
gliding toward earth.
Swinging days
are special days

dipped in fragrance of grass,
caressed with tiptoe breezes,
languidly French-kissed
by the sun.
Days filled with the music of
your laughter,
my love,
and the indignant repertoire of
the nesting mockingbird
up above.

Intruder

I was in the twenties somewhere,
with F. Scott Fitzgerald and Bernice
when suddenly
    there you were
    sloe-eyed and smiling.
I could have scolded—
        should have—
but you were sleepy-giggly
and I was late-night mellow
    so you joined me.
Like two lions lazing in the sun,
we lounged on the couch
    entwined,
sometimes talking, sometimes
    not,

about little things
and life things
and nothings.
And some time in the night,
after popcorn
    and Hershey bars
    and water
    and lots of wiggling
    and a couple of trips to the bathroom,
you fell asleep
and I fell in love
       all over again.

Edgy Sons

"Son, I don't like to see you swinging that shovel."

"Well, close your eyes, Dad!"

—Sam, age three

Morning Reverie

Oh, great. It's 7:30.

Fix your lunch.

Did you finish your homework?

It's due *today?!*

We are *not* having omelets, we're having
Pop-Tarts. We're late.

What do you *mean* you don't have any clean
underwear?

I don't know; I'm in the bathroom.

I don't *know;* I'm in the *bathroom.*

I don't *know!* I'll be out in a *minute!*

Oh, great. No tampons.

Parachutes for the seven dwarves?

What were . . . never mind.

Would the dwarves have needed my *pantyhose,*
   by any chance?
Turn off that television!
Clean up that mess!
You're *still* not dressed?
Don't call your brother names.
You can't wear that.
I don't know! Where were you when you took
   them off?
Somebody get the dog out of the house!
Shut the door!
Oh, great. The gas tank is empty.

Turn down that CD player!

Stop hitting your brother!

Put on that seat belt!

Could you *hush?!* You're driving me *crazy!!*

Don't . . . kick . . . my . . . seat!!!

Well, what do you know? We got here before
    second period.

Okay, bye, babes, have a nice day.

LOVE YA!!

Family Business

Lesson in Economics #1:
If you save half your paycheck every week,
by the time you're twenty,
you'll be halfway to rich.
"I have to work on Saturdays?"
"Do I clock out if I go to the bathroom?"
"Hey! What's FICA and why's it getting all my
    money?"

Lesson in Economics #2:
You can not get paid for work you
do not do.
"But Friday's my birthday! I don't have to work
    on my birthday, do I?"
"I have a headache! You don't expect me to work
    when I'm sick, do you?"
"I'll work extra tomorrow. I gotta see that
    concert tonight!"

Lesson in Economics #3:

It is a cruel, cruel world.

"How could they fire me? I'm the smartest guy there!"

"They're not hiring again till Christmas."

"What do you mean you won't loan me ten bucks?!"

Student Driver

Funny the things you don't notice
till life flashes before your eyes—
like how half the streets in town
are too narrow . . .
like how thirty-five miles per hour
feels waaaaay too fast
when you're in the passenger seat . . .
like how vivid the images can be
when contemplating death
by mailbox impalement.
Take it from one who survived:
far beyond the terrible twos,
light years beyond thirteen,
the Year of the Learner's Permit
is the one that will gray your hair.

No matter how eager
you think you are
to stop schlepping him
all over town . . .
no matter how thrilled
you think you will be
to send him
to the store . . .
no matter how ready
you think you are
to put him
in the driver's seat . . .
you are not.

Chore Wars

I see the weeds have not been pulled,
and the dog has not been fed.
Your dirty socks are *everywhere;*
wet towels are all over your bed.
Your bathroom has reached a new level of low;
I fully expect a citation
for blatant abuse of the state hygiene code
from the Office of Sanitation.
CDs cover the living room floor;
crumbs are all over the couch.
A week's worth of comics are lying there, too,
and you wonder why I'm a grouch?!

I didn't have children in order to serve them:
News Flash—I'm your *mom,* not your maid!
You *will* do your part and you will do it *now!*
I say so, and I *will be obeyed!*

I long for the day you have kids of your own:
my revenge will be so sweet!
I'll tell them *every* disgusting detail—
not a moldy sock will I delete!

But meanwhile, I think more immediate action
is needed and apropos—
some Pavlovian cue that will cause you to
cease and desist your behavior. Sooooo . . .
you are hereby informed that the Gameboy is *mine*—
the Game Cube and Playstation, too.
And until I see no trash, no dirt, and no mess,
the TV and computer are, too!
I'm sorry it had to come to this, dear,
but this time I am truly annoyed.
You should make good use of all your spare time
by inventing a housecleaning droid!

Evil Is Its Name

It's bound to happen.
No matter how hard
you hide the headlines,
shush up the six o'clock news,
recite the rhyme about sticks and stones,
sooner or later
hatred and prejudice will rear their ignorant heads.
Would that the bad guys
always wore black hats, so,
categorically,
like the shepherd dividing the sheep
    and the goats,
you could say, these people are good,
        and these people are bad.
But corruption isn't crowned with a Stetson.
And sadly, the vilest epithets they hear
may come from some
they love.

There's Preacher Jones, who talks the talk
but sorts his flock by surname . . .
Great-Aunt Gwen, whose gender jokes
are always the highlight of bridge club . . .
Mrs. Moore, who bakes for every family
on the street,
except the one she calls "not our kind."
How in the world do you
ever explain Anne Frank,
pro-lifers who kill,
bad cops,
September 11th,
or the four year old who got shot
through the window
while eating his supper last night?
You don't.
You just keep planting flowers
and hope they choke out
the ugly, despicable weeds.

Sibling Rivalry

I love my sister;
she's my best friend.
I love my brother,
and while it's true we rarely
see things eye to eye,
I have never felt a need to
punch him.
Thus it is difficult for me
to comprehend why
blood lust
seems to be the primary emotion
you boys feel for each other.
Were it some Esau-esque birthright
at the heart of the fray—
a ravishing beauty who'd stolen
both your hearts,

the one's noble battle
to prevent the other's act of moral turpitude,
a bitter fight to claim
the only functioning liver left on earth—
perhaps I would understand.
But beating each other up
over Sunday comics?
Fisticuffs over
who occupies the front seat of the car?
Puhleeze!
If it weren't so stupid, it would be
hilarious.
At the moment,
it's anything
but.

Revelation

Sit down,
I have bad news.
I am not always right.
I do not always have the answers,
I can not always fix things.
I may not always know what to do.
But here is the good news:
I will always try.
I will try because I want your way
to be simple.
I want your world to be safe.
I want your life to be filled with
goodness and grace.

All mothers want these things for their sons,
but mothers are not in charge.
So we fight however we can:
with our voices,
our votes,
our valor.
Our ammunition
is love;
our inspiration
is you.

Evolving Sons

It's terrifying to very suddenly be in charge of your own destiny. Still, being free, being out in the real world, is much more exciting than the real world would have you think.

—John, age eighteen

Image Is Everything

We are cool.
Way cool.
Baseball cap, slung sideways,
cemented to hair sheared ear to
here, left Rapunzel-like on top.
Shoes, black, fashionably
loose-laced and flopping,
like clumsy, odoriferous U-boats
gone AWOL on dry land.
Shirt, size mega-large,
blazing retro-neon graphics
The Beav couldn't conjure
in his nastiest nightmare.
Pants, each leg
approaching dirigible girth,
billow ripped and wrinkled
against pale, hairless calves.
We are cool??
Well, we are fifteen.

Inquiring Hearts

Ah, women.
He wants me to explain them.
Young, blonde ones,
in particular.
Well, I'm blonde,
and I was young. . .
but how do I tell him
she'll break his heart?
How do I say
"Be careful!"
without sounding like, well,
a mother?
How do I let him know
there will be many
more blondes—

and likely a brunette or two, as well—
before THE ONE
lays claim to his heart
for good?
Somehow, I think
all he really wants me
to explain
is how to ask Girl #2
to the dance
if Miss Girl of His Dreams
turns him down.

The Fugitive

Where were you running, little boy—
　　toward or away?
Dared by a dancing sunbeam,
lured by a languid frog,
you skipped merrily off
down the summer-dusty road
　　toward adventure, away from mundane.

Where were you running, young man—
　　toward or away?
Dared by a taste of defiance,
lured by a laissez-faire lass,
you slipped stealthily out
into the fog-damp dawn
　　toward fantasy, away from the truth.

Where were you running, mister—
    toward or away?
Dared by a vision of grandeur,
lured by lies you longed to believe,
you strolled haughtily on
past hands stretched out to help
    toward tomorrow, away from today.

Farewell, My Dear One

You wouldn't like it,
I know,
but I've done it for
too many years.
So, taking advantage
of your slumbering senses,
I kiss your forehead,
brush the hair from your brow,
and whisper in your ear
the mantra that's been yours
since birth:
"I love you! I think you're wonderful!
I'm so glad you're my son!"
From those first few nights when
I tiptoed in, holding my breath
to listen for yours,

through nights when you slept,
exhausted,
first from play,
then from living, then
loving.
Now, you lay here
sprawled and tall,
a man's lean, hard body
below my little boy's
soft, sweet face.
Tomorrow, someone else will wake
and kiss you in the night.
So just this once,
I bend and kiss you
twice.

And So You Go

And so you go
out there, to life,
eager to leave the nest,
impatient to spread your wings.
In your face
there is such promise.
In your laugh, such nonchalance.
So much has changed,
yet there are moments—
    subliminal blips—
when I see still the toddler who,
    splayed in my lap or
    head snug against mine,
drank in one story after another,
whispered secrets in the dark,
spilled out kisses and laughs like a beneficent king.

There are moments
      when a pleased expression,
random outburst,
furrowed brow,
brings back a cherished glimpse
of that little boy lost.
In those moments,
it is hardest to say
farewell.
But I must,
and I can,
and I do—
then watch with pride and pain
through tears and years
of love.
And so you go.

Here and There

"You've always been there, Mom."
But we both know I haven't.
I hang up the phone and
a thousand images spin past:
Me not there in preschool:
hysterical sobs and reproving stares
drown my feeble, if valid,
excuse.
Me not there on Field Day:
"Mom! I won third place!"
A moment of pride I missed
while changing your brother's diaper.

Me not there in high school:
you caught a ride and almost died
with your friends in a crash.
Me not there for the play:
"The critics loved me!"
I would have, too,
but what could I do?
Me not there for a birth:
"He's beautiful, Mom!"
I know he is; I'll be there soon!
Me, regardless of where,
always here for you.

Requiem, For My Sons

If I died tomorrow,
contented I would go,
for in my time on earth,
I've had the chance to get to know
your hearts, your minds,
your spirits, and, oh!
what bliss it's been
to watch the world
through your eyes,
see you learning
to be men.

You've shown me courage, laughter,
passion, anguish, pride,
dreams, curiosity, wisdom—
life, personified!
And though I'd long to know
down which path each of you will stray,
I'd take great joy in having gone
along part of the way.

About the Author

Jayne Jaudon Ferrer speaks frequently to women's groups, writers' groups, schools, and civic organizations. If you're interested in scheduling a reading, presentation, or workshop, please visit her website at www.jaynejaudonferrer.com.